S0-BCW-974

JB(Balboa)
Knoop
Vasco Nunez de Balboa

DATE DUE

DEC 4 79
FEB 15 2000

DISCARD

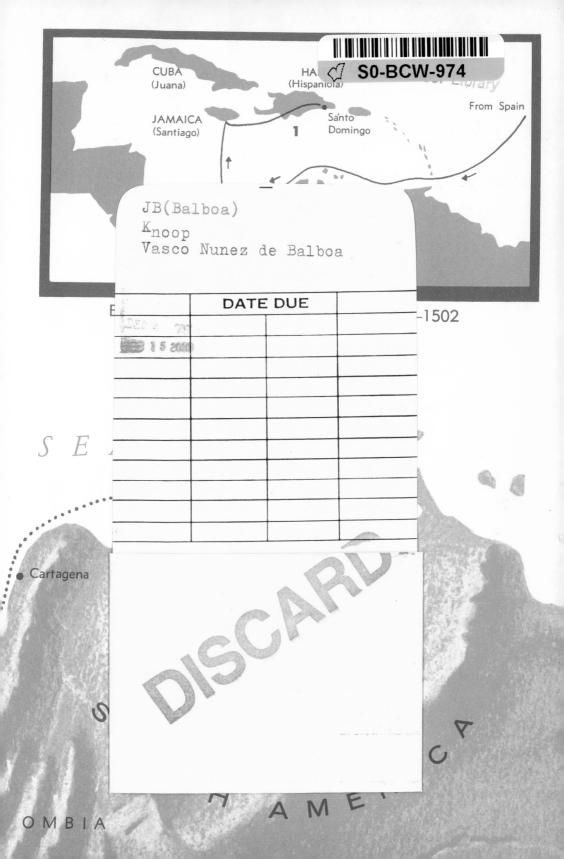

CUBA
(Juana)

HA
(Hispaniola)

JAMAICA
(Santiago)

Santo
Domingo

1

From Spain

–1502

S E

Cartagena

OMBIA

A M E R I C A

THE ASTROLABE, an instrument developed by the Greeks, is the symbol for World Explorer Books. At the time of Columbus, sailors used the astrolabe to chart a ship's course. The arm across the circle could be moved to line up with the sun or a star. Using the number indicated by the pointer, a sailor could tell his approximate location on the sea. Although the astrolabe was not completely accurate, it helped many early explorers in their efforts to conquer the unknown.

World Explorer Books are written especially for children who love adventure and exploration into the unknown. Designed for young readers, each book has been tested by the Dale-Chall readability formula. Leo Fay, Ph.D., Professor of Education at Indiana University, is educational consultant for the series. Dr. Fay, an experienced teacher and lecturer, is well known for his professional bulletins and text material in both elementary reading and social studies.

A WORLD EXPLORER

Vasco Núñez
de Balboa

BY FAITH YINGLING KNOOP

ILLUSTRATED BY VICTOR DOWD

GARRARD PUBLISHING COMPANY
CHAMPAIGN, ILLINOIS

To our youngest
explorer of the sea—
Rebekah Faith

This series is edited by Elizabeth Minot Graves

Copyright © 1969 by Faith Yingling Knoop
All rights reserved. Manufactured in the U.S.A.
Standard Book Number 8116-6464-3
Library of Congress Catalog Card Number: 69-10372

Contents

1. Wooden Swords 5
2. Sword of Steel 9
3. Off to the Indies 15
4. Disappointment in Hispaniola . . 23
5. A Stowaway, a Sword,
    and a Dog 31
6. Mayor Balboa 39
7. Indian Friends 47
8. Troubles in Darien 56
9. Finding an Ocean 63
10. Warrior of the Sun 70
11. Balboa's Worst Enemy 75
12. Ships for the New Sea 82
13. A Good Man's End 90

1

Wooden Swords

The boys' wooden swords flashed in and out. Vasco grinned as he forced his older brother, Gonzalo, back a step. A chair clattered to the courtyard floor.

The noise brought the boys' mother to a doorway framed by climbing roses. It was a warm spring day in 1486. "Vasco Núñez de Balboa!" his mother cried. "You've torn your doublet again!"

Vasco looked at his torn right sleeve. "I'm sorry," he said. His face turned nearly as red as his red-gold hair. "I asked Gonzalo to teach me a new sword stroke."

"I'm sorry, too, Mother," Gonzalo added. "I can't teach Vasco much, anyway. He wins half of our duels, though he is only eleven."

Father Nuño Arias de Balboa appeared in the doorway. Little Juan, the youngest of his three sons, peeped from behind him. "Boys," ordered their father, "I want to talk to you."

"About tearing my new doublet?" Vasco asked sadly, as his parents sat down on a carved bench.

Don Nuño smiled. "You are hard on your clothes, Vasco. You grow so fast and are so active." He shook his head, then went on. "I wrote to my old friend, Don Pedro Puertocarrero, about you. He is Lord of Moguer, you know." The Balboas lived in Jerez de los Caballeros, a town in western Spain. Moguer was near the Atlantic Ocean, 80 miles away.

Vasco's blue eyes shone. "Will he take me as a page when I'm twelve?" he asked.

Don Nuño Arias de Balboa put a hand on his second son's shoulder. "I told Don Pedro how strong and tall you are. He will train you now. You may join a group of travelers going to Moguer this very week."

Vasco jumped up, waving his wooden sword. "A page! Then a squire! Then a knight and a king's soldier!" he shouted happily.

Vasco's eyes fell on his mother's sad face. He knelt beside her and felt her gentle hand on his head. "I'll miss you all," he said, "but I'll make you proud of me."

"How lucky you are, Vasco," Gonzalo broke in. "I almost wish I weren't the oldest son. I must stay home and help Father take care of our property."

"I'm sure all my boys will honor the Balboa name," Father nodded. "Our family is not as rich and powerful as it once was. But remember this: Balboas are of royal blood. They have been knights, governors, and doctors. They have held high church titles and have been advisors to kings."

Vasco's dancing blue eyes grew thoughtful. "I'll remember," he promised. He stood up, holding his sword like a knight. "I shall do some great deed some day, to make the world remember us all."

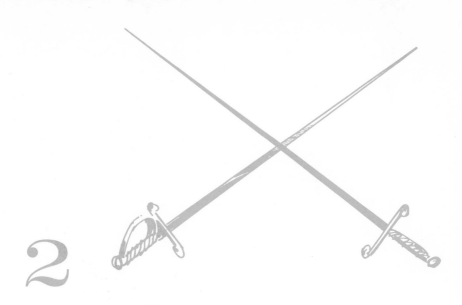

Sword of Steel

"The castle!" shouted Vasco to the other travelers on the road to Moguer. He was the first to see the great stone towers ahead. "My new home," he added to himself.

Time flew fast in the castle of Moguer. Vasco and the other pages studied geography and arithmetic, letter writing and good manners. Their teacher was the castle priest, kind Friar Juan. The boys waited on the knights and ran errands.

They learned to wrestle, swim, and use their pages' daggers. Everyone liked cheerful, redheaded Vasco Núñez de Balboa.

When he was fourteen, Vasco became a squire. He knelt before Don Pedro, Lord of Moguer, and handed the Lord his page's dagger. Don Pedro gave Vasco a new steel sword for his very own. Vasco stood, holding it proudly in his right hand. He promised, "I will always be true to my King and my God. I will be honest and fair with friend and foe."

Squires learned horseback riding, hunting, and fighting with the lance and sword. Soon tall Vasco could defeat every other squire in sword practice. He was ready to be a knight's assistant in battle. The squires all hoped to fight in Spain's Moorish War.

The African Moors had invaded Spain

nearly 800 years before. They had ruled part of the country ever since, in spite of constant wars against them. Now Queen Isabella and King Ferdinand had united all of Spain to drive the Africans from Spanish ground.

At seventeen, Vasco was still in Moguer. "When can I fight the Moors?" he asked Friar Juan one day.

"The Moors will soon surrender their capital at Granada," the Friar answered. "The King needs no more soldiers there."

Vasco's blue eyes fell. "I would die for my King and country," he said.

"It matters more to live for one's country," the Friar replied gently.

"How?" Vasco shrugged.

"By finding a quick sea route to India," Friar Juan answered. "The Turks block our overland travel to Asia. Their taxes

on Asia's spices and drugs, and silks and jewels are too high." He broke off, to ask Vasco, "Have you heard of Christopher Columbus?"

"An Italian seaman?" asked Vasco. "Somebody with a crazy idea of sailing west to reach the East?"

Friar Juan smiled. "Not crazy, perhaps. Scientists already believe the earth to be round. Columbus asks the King and

Queen for ships to sail west across the Ocean Sea, to India. If Spain is first to find that way to Asia, and her gold and spices . . . ."

"What adventure!" Vasco broke in. "I'll go with Columbus."

Soon Vasco heard that three ships were being outfitted for Columbus in the nearby port of Palos. Vasco went to Palos hoping to join the expedition.

But Columbus needed seamen, not soldiers. Disappointed, Vasco waved good-bye as Columbus' ships sailed from Spain in August, 1492.

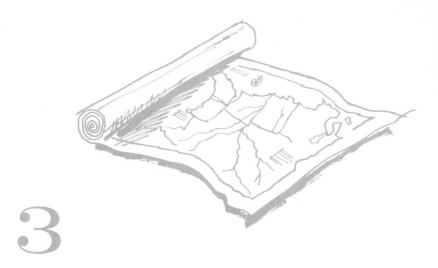

3

Off to the Indies

"Land! Land!" Vasco Núñez de Balboa, now 26, joined in the sailors' glad cry. At last he had crossed the Ocean Sea.

It was 1501, nine years after Columbus' discovery of the Indies—islands that he thought lay near India. Balboa, one of the best swordsmen in Spain, was guarding the expedition of Rodrigo de Bastidas with five other soldiers. The explorers had just sighted a small Caribbean island.

"We cannot stop here," Captain De Bastidas told his men. "King Ferdinand's orders are to trade and explore in lands not yet discovered by Spain."

"There will be more treasure in the new lands ahead," Balboa said, "and more adventure." What riches he would send his parents and brothers in Spain!

Bastidas' two ships sailed along the northern coast of South America. "We call this the 'Pearl Coast,'" the ship's pilot told Balboa. Pilot Juan de la Cosa had once sailed with Columbus. Later he had piloted the explorer Alonso de Ojeda to the Indies.

The explorers soon reached the Gulf of Venezuela, so named by Ojeda. "No European has ever sailed past this gulf," De la Cosa announced. So Bastidas anchored his ships just beyond it.

"Row the landing boat to the beach," Bastidas ordered his soldiers. "Take some trinkets to trade with the natives."

A crowd of unfriendly Indians gathered on the shore. They blew seashell horns. They yelled and spat, trying to scare the strangers away.

But Balboa and his men waded bravely ashore from the landing boat. They held up strings of beads, tiny round bells, mirrors, and bright cloth. Suddenly an Indian reached for a bell. Balboa pointed to the Indian's gold jewelry. Soon the Spaniards' bells were being traded for gold and pearls.

The expedition continued along the coast, trading peacefully with the natives. Then one day some Indians shot arrows at the Spanish ships. "Leave these Indians alone," Juan de la Cosa warned. "They may have poisoned arrows." He turned the ships into the Gulf of Urabá, close to today's Central America.

Here the Indians were friendly. They brought great baskets of gold and pearls to trade. "We will all be rich!" Balboa cried.

The ships followed the coast, trading as they went. One day Balboa carried a treasure chest down into the ship's hold. The hold was full of water. Balboa called Pilot De la Cosa.

The pilot shook his head. "Tropical shipworms are eating the ship's hull," he said sadly. "We must sail to the island of Jamaica. The trees there make fine ships' timbers. We'll repair our ships there."

It was February, 1502, by the time the ships were repaired. "Sail for Spain,"

Captain Bastidas ordered. They neared the island of Hispaniola, which had been settled by Columbus. Suddenly a terrible storm arose. The ships were wrecked on the island's rocky shore, near today's Port-au-Prince, Haiti.

Balboa led the men as they waded through the fierce waves with the treasure chests. The castaways flung themselves onto the beach to rest. "What good is

our gold here?" one half-drowned sailor worried. "We should have saved food."

Pilot Juan de la Cosa stood up. "Santo Domingo, capital of Hispaniola, is 200 miles away," he told the men. "I will lead you there."

"We have been forbidden to land on Hispaniola, for it is already settled," Bastidas frowned. "Santo Domingo may turn us away."

"Surely the Spaniards there will pity other Spaniards in trouble," Balboa answered cheerfully.

The hike proved a terrible one and took weeks. The castaways had to cross steep mountains in the middle of the island. Then they trudged along the swampy coast. Many explorers died of starvation, or fever. Others died from accidents. Yet Balboa and the strongest men carried the treasure chests all the way to Santo Domingo.

Then, at the city gate, an angry guard cried, "Halt! Anybody without a pass is under arrest!"

Disappointment in Hispaniola

"Now we have food and a roof over our heads," Balboa grinned. The castaways were locked in Santo Domingo's jail.

A month later, the men were freed. Captain Bastidas and Pilot De la Cosa were sent to Spain to be tried for landing on Hispaniola. Bastidas took all the treasure with him.

"We'll have to make our fortunes with some other expedition," Balboa told his disappointed companions. "Until then, I am joining the army here."

Balboa found army life in Hispaniola quite different from knights' service in Spain. His troops were sent into the mountains to collect taxes of gold from the Indians. When the natives had no gold, they were seized for slaves. Some were sent to Spain to be sold. Others were put to work in Hispaniola, building or farming. Unarmed Indians who resisted were killed.

Balboa disliked the Spaniards' senseless cruelty and returned to Santo Domingo. He asked Captain Ponce de Leon for his army pay.

The captain, who later became famous for discovering Florida, answered sadly, "Your pay is not money, but farm land in southwest Hispaniola. You will have

Indians to work it. You can raise pigs.
Santo Domingo needs pork."

"Pigs!" Balboa's blue eyes flashed. "I
am no swineherd."

Ponce de Leon smiled, "Come," he said.
"I have something else for you."

Balboa followed the captain into a
courtyard. De Leon's fierce war dog,
Becerillo, was tied there. Nearby was a
litter of tiny yellow puppies. De Leon
handed one to Balboa saying, "He's yours."

The puppy wagged his tail and licked Balboa's hand. Balboa laughed. "I shall call him Leoncico, 'little lion,' for you, Captain De Leon," he said. "Thank you."

On his faraway farm, Balboa worked with his Indians clearing land. They built a cottage and fenced the fields. Then there was nothing to do but watch pigs.

One day Balboa leaped from his hammock saying, "What are we doing here, Leoncico? A war dog and a soldier! Let's go back to Santo Domingo." And back they went, leaving the farm and pigs to the Indians.

Santo Domingo was crowded with penniless young noblemen from Spain. All were seeking fortunes of gold in the Indies. There were not enough houses or work for them. Balboa and many others had to borrow money just to eat.

No new expeditions were setting out at this time. For the Spanish King had ruled that explorers must pay for their own voyages, without royal help. King Ferdinand was disappointed in the little treasure received from the Indies. Indeed, many Europeans now realized this was not a rich Asian land, after all, but a New World with little gold. Rich people feared to risk lending money to explorers.

Several years passed. Then one day a crier shouted through the streets of Santo Domingo, "The King sends Alonso de Ojeda and Diego de Nicuesa to settle and govern the mainland discovered by Captain Bastidas!"

Balboa hurried to the waterfront with his friend Bartolomé Hurtado. Hurtado was a stocky young soldier whom Balboa had met in Hispaniola. They found the

two governors signing up men for their expeditions.

"I shall govern the coast east of the Gulf of Urabá," short, handsome Alonso announced. "My pilot is Juan de la Cosa."

"De la Cosa, my old friend, is the best pilot in the world," Balboa told Hurtado. "Let us sign up with Alonso." They did not even listen to rich, swaggering Nicuesa. He was to rule the land north-west of the Gulf of Urabá.

Alonso sailed on December 13, 1509, with 220 men. But neither Balboa nor Hurtado was among them. Balboa owed much money, and a new law forbade debtors to leave Hispaniola until their debts were paid. Hurtado did not want to go without Balboa.

Sadly the two friends watched Alonso's three ships start down the Ozama River to the Caribbean. "Alonso's partner, the lawyer Enciso, will join him later with more men and supplies," Hurtado said. "Perhaps we can sail then."

Balboa's eyes brightened. "Yes," he answered. "I have an idea." He began to whisper to Hurtado.

A few days later, Balboa and Hurtado saw Nicuesa's seven ships set out with 700 men. The two friends smiled. They had a plan to make it possible for Balboa to sail with Enciso.

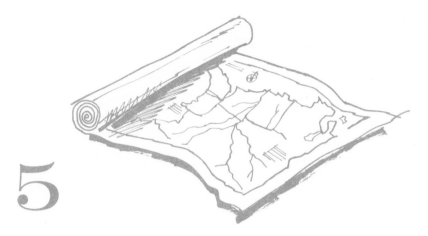

5

A Stowaway, a Sword, and a Dog

Bells rang. Trumpets sounded. People cheered from the Santo Domingo wharf. It was September, 1510. Enciso's two supply ships were sailing to join Alonso de Ojeda on the South American coast. They carried 150 men, including friars to teach the Indians about Christianity.

Balboa, still in debt, had been forbidden to sail. Hurtado stood on the flagship's deck, beside a huge flour barrel. A strange, bumping noise came from the barrel. The sailors looked at it curiously.

When they were at sea, Hurtado ordered the sailors to open the barrel. Out jumped tall Vasco Núñez de Balboa, sword in hand. His dog, Leoncico, followed. The sailors roared with laughter.

Short, fat lawyer Enciso strutted into the crowd. He stamped his foot in rage. "No debtor sails with me!" he screamed. "Throw Balboa onto yonder desert island!"

The sailors did not move. "Please, sir," Hurtado saluted his employer, "Balboa is the only man here who has explored the mainland we seek."

"I must earn my fortune to pay my debts," Balboa answered softly, fingering his sword. Leoncico growled at Enciso.

Balboa and Leoncico stayed.

Soon Balboa pointed out the South

American coast discovered on his former expedition. Enciso's ships stopped for water near today's Cartagena, Colombia.

Suddenly another ship appeared. "We are from Alonso de Ojeda's expedition," a voice shouted. "Pizarro is our captain."

Black-haired, black-bearded Francisco Pizarro had been a swineherd in Spain. He could not read or write, but he was fierce and fearless in battle. He led 41 thin, starving men ashore. "Food!" they begged.

Balboa and his companions watched with pity as the sick men ate wolfishly.

Pizarro told about Alonso's expedition. "The Indians fought us wherever we sought gold," Pizzaro said. "They shot poisoned arrows. Pilot Juan de la Cosa was killed at our first landing. Later we built a fort on the east coast of the Gulf of Urabá, hoping to start a settlement. Alonso named it Fort San Sebastián."

"Where is Governor Alonso?" Enciso broke in sharply.

"Indians besieged our fort," Pizarro explained. "They kept us from getting food in the forest when our supplies gave out. One day a stray ship came and traded some food for gold. Alonso sailed away on that ship to get help in Santo Domingo. He left me in charge of the fort."

Pizarro chewed greedily, before going on. "We waited 50 days for help. None came. Every day men died of starvation. Finally we set out in two ships, hoping to reach Santo Domingo."

"Two ships?" asked Enciso.

"One sank with everyone on board," Pizarro sighed. "We are the only ones left of Alonso's 220 men."

"Then I am your commander," Enciso declared, "for I am Alonso's partner. You shall return to San Sebastián with us, to subdue the Indians." Grumbling, Pizarro's men had to obey.

As they neared San Sebastián, the Spaniards saw that the fort was in ruins. Indians had burned it to the ground. "Do not go any closer to land," Balboa warned Enciso. "This water is too shallow for our flagship."

Enciso paid no attention. Suddenly the flagship ran onto sharp rocks. It sank. The men and Leoncico swam to shore with a few supplies. All of the livestock and most of the food were lost.

Enciso at once ordered 100 soldiers to raid the nearest Indian village for food and gold. Balboa and Pizarro stayed on the beach, guarding the supplies. Soon

they saw the 100 Spaniards racing back, chased by three Indians. The Indians were shooting poisoned arrows.

Balboa took charge of the frightened men. "We traded across the gulf on my other voyage," he said. "The Indians there do not have poisoned arrows."

"Let's cross the gulf!" the soldiers shouted.

"That land is Governor Nicuesa's," Enciso protested.

Balboa shrugged. "If so, we will join him. Staying here means starvation, or death by poisoned arrows."

6

Mayor Balboa

The Spaniards sailed across the Gulf of Urabá. The land there was then called Darien. There were no signs of Governor Nicuesa.

Balboa and Leoncico led the men up the Darien River. Suddenly they came upon an Indian village guarded by 500 warriors.

"Santiago!" Enciso shouted the Spanish war cry. The Spaniards charged, and the natives fled into the jungle.

Remembering his first voyage, Balboa sighed. The Darien Indians had traded peacefully with the explorers then. The Spaniards should make friends with the Indians if Spain were to settle this land.

Instead, the greedy Spaniards swarmed into the Indians' shacks, stealing food and gold ornaments. "Pile the gold together!" Enciso ordered. "It is mine. I paid for the expedition."

The men faced Enciso angrily. "It is the law," Balboa said quietly, "to set aside a fifth of all treasure for the King. The rest is then divided among the explorers."

"Alonso left me in charge," Pizarro muttered to a friend. "But Enciso and Balboa are taking over."

Enciso did not hear Pizarro. He glared at Balboa, but did not dare to take the treasure. He turned away to give other orders. "We will build a town here," he said, "and name it 'Santa Maria del Antigua del Darien.' "

Santa Maria was started at once, beside the Indian village. It was the first town built by Europeans on the American mainland. It was in what is now Colombia near the Panama border, a few miles from the sea. Misty mountains rose behind the town.

Soon some Indians returned from the jungle. They began working for the Spaniards and learned to speak Spanish.

Balboa directed the building of a church, a fort, and some houses. He helped clear more land for beans and squash beside the Indians' cornfields. Enciso strutted about the town, all the while shouting orders and angering everyone.

At last the settlers held a secret meeting. "If this is really Governor Nicuesa's land," they said, "the lawyer Enciso is not in charge here. We must elect other officers." They chose Balboa as mayor. Enciso was furious. So was Pizarro, who had hoped to be mayor.

Soon afterward, Hurtado told Balboa, "Beware of Enciso and Pizarro. They are both terribly jealous. They will do anything to crush you."

Balboa shrugged. "I do not fear them. They were glad enough to follow me away from San Sebastián."

Hurtado shook his head. "You are honest and hold no grudges," he answered. "You do not understand mean men who live only for gold and power."

Just then a messenger ran into the clearing. He had come from the nearby harbor on the coast. "A ship!" he cried. "A food ship has just arrived, seeking Governor Nicuesa!"

Mayor Balboa hurried to the harbor to see the ship's captain. "Nicuesa must be far up the coast," Balboa explained. "Have you any news of Governor Alonso de Ojeda?"

The answer was, "No."

The settlers decided then to send messengers to Nicuesa aboard the food ship. They would ask him to come to Santa Maria and govern it along with his own colony.

A few weeks later, the messengers brought back word of Nicuesa. "He is many miles away," they reported. "Only 65 of his 700 men are still alive, and these men were starving before the ship brought food. When Governor Nicuesa

learned about Santa Maria and our invitation to join us, he claimed the town and all its gold. He is coming here now to take charge."

"No, no!" shouted the settlers. "It is our gold."

Nicuesa soon appeared in a small, leaky ship. The settlers lined up on their beach. As Nicuesa was rowed from the ship to shore, the settlers roared, "Turn back!"

Nicuesa, pale and scared, begged for mercy. Balboa advised his people, "Let them land."

But his men would not obey. They waved their swords wildly. Nicuesa was rowed back to his ship.

Behind the other settlers, Lawyer Enciso smiled slyly. He wondered if the frail boat would not soon sink with all on board. "If so," he thought, "Balboa will be blamed for Nicuesa's drowning, and punished by the King." Sure enough, Nicuesa was never seen again.

Soon afterward, Santa Maria's best ship left for Santo Domingo. Its precious load of treasure would be sent on to Spain. The ship also carried important letters. The settlers had written to Governor Diego Columbus in Hispaniola and King Ferdinand in Spain. They asked that Balboa be appointed Governor of Darien. They asked for more men and building supplies too.

The ship sailed away with Balboa's friends on board, and one enemy—Lawyer Enciso.

7

Indian Friends

Santa Maria's buildings were finished. "Now it is time to explore," Balboa told his men. "Our Indian servants tell of a rich land to the northwest, called 'Careta.' They will lead us there.

"Remember, the King's orders are to trade peacefully with the natives unless they attack. We are to claim new land and people for Spain. We shall teach the Indians about our Bible, as well as find treasure."

Before exploring Careta, Balboa sent Pizarro on a short scouting trip. Pizarro returned with only four of his five men. "The Indians beat us off when we attacked," Pizarro reported. "Hernando fell wounded in the forest."

"I did not order an attack on anyone," Balboa snapped. "Take a stretcher and bring Hernando back."

Balboa himself tended the wounded man, who recovered. Pizarro, angry at being scolded, hated Balboa more than ever.

Balboa started up the coast with 80 men. Hurtado, Pizarro, and two friars were among them. Leoncico trotted beside his master.

Careta was in what is now Panama, on the Caribbean Sea. The Spaniards were met there by a battle line of Indians.

Balboa sank his sword into the ground and held out his open hands. The chief threw down his war club. Indians and Spaniards were friends.

The Caretan Indians gladly traded gold ornaments for bells and axes. Their chief became a Christian. He asked Balboa to bring up his ten-year-old daughter as a Spaniard. And he told Balboa about Comogra, 140 miles beyond Careta. "It is the richest land of all," he said. "My men will lead you there."

So the Spaniards set out for Comogra. There were hostile Indians along the way. But most of them surrendered at their first sight of the Spaniards' tall leader and his yellow war dog. If an Indian attacked, nothing could save him from Leoncico's fangs. But Leoncico sensed which Indian runaways were ready to surrender. He led them gently to his master by their hands.

"Leoncico is one of us," the soldiers said. The dog was given a soldier's pay and a golden collar.

At last the explorers reached Comogra, in the mountains by the sea. Its chief gave Balboa a heavy golden chain that was ten feet long. He invited the Spaniards into his huge, carved wooden

palace. Its inner room, called the "Hall of Ancestors," held rows of royal mummies. They were covered with rich cloth and gold and pearls. The visitors gasped in wonder.

Comogra's chief loaded his guests with golden ornaments. Then the Spaniards' greed overcame their manners. They set up scales to weigh the gold. They talked about melting it into bars to ship to Spain. The Spaniards' guides translated this to the Comograns.

Suddenly sixteen-year-old Ponquiaco, the chief's oldest son, struck the scales and gold to the ground. "You destroy the beauty of gold jewelry by melting it," he cried scornfully. "If you want only golden chunks, I can show you the land where it grows in the streams."

"Where?" yelled the Spaniards.

"Four days' march from here, on the Other Sea," Ponquiaco answered. "But you will need 1,000 soldiers to overcome the cannibals on the way."

"Gold! Gold!" The Spaniards went mad with excitement.

Balboa stood aside, thinking. He knew that Columbus' "India" was probably a new continent. If so, the "Other Sea" could be the Indian Ocean south of Asia! Its finder would be famous forever.

Balboa quieted his men. "We shall return to Santa Maria with our treasure," he ordered. "Then we'll plan an expedition to the Other Sea."

The Spaniards marched back into Santa Maria after six months of exploring. They were greeted with cheers and exciting news.

A shipload of food and men had just

arrived from Santo Domingo. There was word of Governor Alonso de Ojeda. After leaving Fort San Sebastián, he had been shipwrecked on Cuba's deserted coast. He was now in Santo Domingo. Lame and ill, he wanted no more exploring.

Governor Nicuesa had never been seen again after leaving Santa Maria. So Governor Columbus had named Balboa Captain of Darien. King Ferdinand had yet to approve the appointment.

Captain Balboa of Darien wrote to the King at once. He asked for 1,000 trained soldiers to explore the land of gold on the Other Sea.

8

Troubles in Darien

Balboa and Hurtado watched a graceful ship sail from Santa Maria's harbor. "It carries more gold and pearls for the King than ever were sent before," Balboa said proudly. "My own share can pay my debts and help my family in Spain too."

Hurtado had a worried frown. "We ourselves need help," he reminded Balboa. "We need supplies from Santo Domingo. That last hurricane destroyed our new crops. The food in our storehouse is almost gone."

"You worry too much, Hurtado," Balboa laughed. "Everything will be all right."

But everything went wrong in Darien, that year of 1512. The treasure ship was lost at sea. No food came from Santo Domingo. As the crops of the Indians near Santa Maria had also failed, the settlers began to starve.

"We must get food from the Indians to the south," Balboa decided. The warlike Indians south of Santa Maria had never been won over by trading, or by war. Balboa led his best soldiers south, wearing their heaviest armor. On the march, the Spaniards' only foods were wild fruits, birds, and great iguana lizards.

The southern Indians fought off the invaders fiercely. Only one tribe that lived

in tree houses was conquered when the Spaniards cut down their trees. But these Indians had little food. Balboa's men returned to Santa Maria empty handed. New crops planted there were not yet ripe. Everyone was very hungry.

One day an Indian servant warned Balboa, "Four southern tribes plot to wipe out Santa Maria. They plan to kill you first, Master, when you inspect your cornfield tomorrow. Do not go!"

But Balboa rode out to the cornfield as usual. Leoncico ran along beside the horse. Suddenly an Indian crept up to Captain Balboa. The Captain's red-gold hair shone in the sun like a crown. The sword at his side flashed. Leoncico growled fiercely.

The Indian turned and ran in fear. He was followed by 40 other warriors who had been hiding in nearby bushes. Their plot had failed.

Soon there was another plot. A dozen of Balboa's own men planned to steal the colony's gold from the storehouse. Hurtado learned of the plan and told Balboa. The traitors were jailed in a great wooden cage in the town square. When they promised to be loyal, Balboa agreed to free them.

"You should not free them," Hurtado warned Balboa in vain. "They will work with Pizarro to overthrow you."

Finally the unlucky year ended. In late December, 1512, two ships arrived from Santo Domingo with food. Balboa wrote the King, "If they had come any later, there would have been none left here to be fed." He again asked for more men to explore the Other Sea.

In June, Balboa received the King's appointment as Captain and Governor of Darien. His dreams seemed to be coming true. But the very next ship brought a warning letter from a friend in Spain.

"Enciso has turned the King against you," the friend wrote. "He claims that you sent Nicuesa away in a leaky ship to drown. The King is going to send a new governor to Darien to replace you."

Balboa's blue eyes blazed with anger. "I have planned for almost two years to find the Other Sea," he stormed. "No new governor shall cheat me of my discovery. I shall not wait for more soldiers. A hundred of my own men are worth 1,000 new troops!"

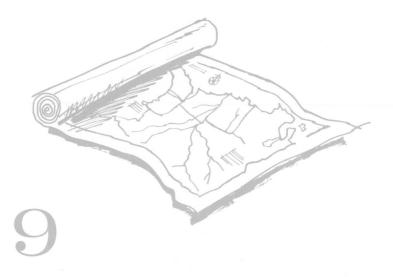

9

Finding an Ocean

"To the land of gold!" shouted 190 soldiers.

"To the Other Sea!" added Balboa and the two friars on the expedition. This time, they were sailing up the coast to Careta, instead of marching by land. The trail to the Other Sea began there.

In Careta, Balboa set up a rest camp and supply base. Then he chose 94 men to start off for the Other Sea. Among them were Pizarro, Hurtado, and the friars. Pizarro was a good soldier—but needed watching.

Leoncico led a pack of war dogs. Several hundred Caretan Indians were bearers and guides for the 50-mile march.

The army's single line strung out for a half mile on the narrow mountain path. Soldiers sang. Indians blew reed whistles. Dogs barked. The expedition was on its way.

The trail grew steep. Songs changed to groans. The sweating army crossed ravines on swinging vine bridges. Balancing their belongings on shields on their heads, the Spaniards waded swift rivers. The water was often up to their necks. Many men fell sick with tropical fevers. The Indians carried the sick back to camp on stretchers made of spears and shirts. Tired Caretans were replaced by fresh bearers along the way.

The trail led onto a high, cool plateau. Here fiercely painted Indians barred the way. "They are cannibals!" a scout told Balboa.

"Santiago!" shouted Balboa. The soldiers and war dogs charged. Swords, dogs, and crossbows mowed down the enemy. At their chief's death, the Indians surrendered. They brought gold ornaments to the conquerors. The Spaniards marched on.

On September 25, 1513, three weeks after leaving Careta, a guide pointed to a rocky mountaintop. "From there, you can see the Other Sea," he said.

Nothing could slow Balboa now. He strode ahead of his men, Leoncico beside him. Man and dog panted up the mountain to its peak. There Balboa shaded his eyes, looking south. He saw an endless blue sea with sparkling waves. The Other Sea! He fell to his knees, thanking God for his great discovery. Then he shouted to his lagging men. Only 67 were left, of the 94 who had started.

At Balboa's shout, the Spaniards scrambled up the mountain. Sighting the ocean, they, too, knelt. "I claim this Other Sea for Spain!" Balboa declared.

A tall tree was felled and set up, shaped like a cross. The friars prayed. All Spanish discoveries were made in the name of God as well as in that of the King. Hymns were sung. The discoverers marched on toward the distant sea, still singing.

Four days later the Spaniards reached

a gulf of the South Sea, as they had named the water. Balboa chose 26 of his leaders for a ceremony to honor their great discovery. Wearing their best armor, they paraded to the seashore.

The tide was out, leaving an oozing swamp between shore and water. Balboa waited for the tide to turn before shouting, "Forward!" He waded into the sea, waving a bright Spanish banner in one hand. His sword gleamed high in the other hand. Leoncico splashed and swam beside his master. The 26 men followed into the surf, Hurtado and Pizarro among them.

Balboa's helmet plumes fluttered above his shining armor. "I take possession of these seas, lands, and islands for the royal Crown of Spain!" he announced. "I promise to defend these discoveries against attacks by land or sea." His men repeated the pledge. "I name this bay the Gulf of San Miguel of the South Sea," Balboa ended.

Now Captain Balboa and his men tasted the water from their cupped hands. They smacked their lips, saying, "It is salt, like the other oceans!" The ceremony was over. Balboa had claimed the whole Pacific Ocean and its shores and islands for Spain.

10

Warrior of the Sun

"We must map the coast," Balboa told his men, "before returning to Santa Maria." To Balboa, now 38, exploring for Spain had become more important than gold. His mind buzzed with questions. What lay beyond this unknown sea and along its shores? But his men wanted only treasure.

The Spaniards marched northwest exploring the Pacific coast of today's

Panama. Everywhere the natives welcomed them with gifts of gold and pearls. "The strangers may be white gods," some Indians said. They called Balboa, with his red hair and beard, "Warrior of the Sun."

An Indian prince pointed out the Pearl Islands, 25 miles from shore. "Our canoes cannot reach the islands in this stormy season," he told Balboa. "But in three months, we'll get you hundreds of pearls." Balboa marvelled at some canoe paddles studded with pearls, but could not wait. The Spaniards pressed on.

The soldiers asked each tribe, "Where are your gold streams?" Usually the Indians made signs showing that little gold remained in their streams. Then they would point south.

At last a wise old chief told Balboa,

"The true Golden Kingdom is far south
beside this sea. There men walk on gold
floors. They have beasts of burden like
this." He molded clay into a long-necked
animal. It was the first time that Europeans
ever heard of Peru's llamas. Balboa wondered if they were the camels of Asia.

"We must return here with shipbuild-
ing supplies," Balboa told his men. "We
need ships to reach the Pearl Islands and
the Golden Kingdom." He led his men

into the mountains to circle back to Careta. They had to fight more cannibal tribes on the way. Many soldiers were now ill with tropical fever. Even strong Balboa fell sick and had to be carried in a hammock hung from a long pole.

At last the weary explorers reached Comogra, the rich country with the gold-trimmed mummies. The old chief was dead, and his son, Ponquiaco, ruled the land. It was Ponquiaco who had first told the explorers about the Other Sea. He welcomed the Spaniards, and they rested in Comogra for five days. Here Balboa traded axes and his best shirt for more gold.

By the time the explorers reached Careta, they had won 30 Indian tribes as allies of Spain. Most of these tribes were won by trading, not fighting.

Balboa sailed at once for Santa Maria. He arrived there on January 19, 1514, nearly five months after setting out. The settlers could hardly believe their eyes at the sight of the expedition's treasure.

Captain Balboa hurried to write King Ferdinand about this discovery. "Surely, now the King will leave me in charge here," he told Hurtado.

But Hurtado still worried, "If only his Highness gets your report before sending another governor to Darien!"

11

Balboa's Worst Enemy

The following June, a messenger raced into Santa Maria. "An armada of more than 20 ships has anchored in the harbor!" he shouted. "They bring settlers—and a new governor!" As Hurtado had feared, the King had not learned of Balboa's discovery in time. He had sent Pedrarias de Avila, a long-time army officer, to rule the colony.

Balboa tried not to show his disappointment, as he led his men down the jungle path to welcome the newcomers. The veterans stared in wonder at the people walking toward them. There were 2,000 men, women, and children, all dressed in silks and satins as if for a king's ball. They were headed by Bishop Quevedo in purple velvet.

Balboa knelt before the tall, black-haired bishop. Then he rose and bowed to fat, big-nosed Pedrarias. The new governor's hair had once been red like Balboa's, but was now streaked with gray. Pedrarias was nearly 70 years old. His young wife, Isabel, was beside him. Lawyer Enciso, Balboa's enemy, was also there.

Pedrarias handed Balboa the King's orders. "I am Governor of all of Castillo

del Oro (Castle of Gold)," he announced. "That is the new name for Spain's mainland here." Castillo del Oro covered most of the Caribbean coasts of today's Colombia and Panama.

Balboa read the orders.

Pedrarias went on, "I am to find the Other Sea."

"Welcome," returned Balboa politely. "We have already discovered the South Sea and explored its coast."

Pedrarias' little green eyes blazed with anger. He had lost the chance of a great discovery. "Take us to our new homes," he ordered.

Santa Maria had 200 houses and over 500 people. Some new houses were being built. But Balboa had not known how many new settlers were coming, nor when. Pedrarias, seeing so few houses, flew into a rage. He blamed Balboa and ordered him not to leave Santa Maria.

"But I must build ships to explore the South Sea and find the Golden Kingdom," Balboa cried.

"You cannot leave Santa Maria," Pedrarias repeated.

Soon a terrible disease struck the newcomers. Seven hundred of them died within two months. Hundreds of others returned to Spain by the ships that had brought them.

Enough new soldiers stayed, however, to carry out Pedrarias' cruel orders. They plundered the Indian villages for gold. Enciso and Pizarro led the looting. Balboa's Indian friends were killed or enslaved. Balboa, held in Santa Maria, was unable to help his friends, for Pedrarias' word was law.

Months passed. Then an Italian astronomer, Micer Codro, came to Santa Maria to study the stars. One night he warned Balboa, "When yonder star is between those others, your life will be in danger."

Balboa laughed, "My life is in danger every day."

One sad day, Leoncico was found dead. The dog had been poisoned by one of Pedrarias' Spanish servants. Balboa never learned the poisoner's name.

In the spring of 1515, mail arrived from Spain. At first, Pedrarias held back two letters for Balboa. They were from the King.

When Balboa finally was allowed to read them, he smiled. "You and your men will be well rewarded," the King had written. "Everything you have undertaken, you have done very well."

The King appointed Balboa *Adelantado*, or Ruler, of the South Sea coast, which he had discovered. He was also made Governor of Careta, and the land between it and the South Sea.

But Balboa's lands were a part of the great Castillo del Oro, still ruled by Pedrarias. Balboa was still under the command of his enemy.

12

Ships for the New Sea

Pedrarias refused to give Balboa any men for his new land. So Balboa had to remain in Santa Maria another year. Then one glad day, 60 soldiers arrived from Santo Domingo. "We come to explore the South Sea with Balboa," their leader announced.

Balboa laughed for joy.

But the "Fury," as Governor Pedrarias was now called, flew into another rage. "Balboa tries to overthrow me!" he shouted. "Arrest him!" Balboa was jailed in a wooden cage in Pedrarias' courtyard.

Luckily, Pedrarias' wife and Bishop Quevedo were Balboa's friends. They warned Pedrarias that Balboa's arrest would anger the King. And they arranged an engagement between Maria de Avila, the Governor's daughter in Spain, and Balboa. Balboa had never met Maria, but he agreed to marry her.

Pedrarias then freed Balboa. "My son, go to Careta," he said. "Build a town there, then explore the South Sea."

In August, 1516, Balboa and Hurtado headed for Careta with 175 men. They built a town on an old Indian battle-ground called Acla or "Bones of the

Dead." Then they cut timbers to carry over the mountains. The timbers would be used in building ships to explore the South Sea, for the Indians said that shipworms never ate Careta's wood.

A long line of Spaniards and Indian bearers set out along the hot jungle trail. They carried ships' timbers, sails, nails, anchors, and instruments. Across the rivers they went, through swamps and over mountain passes. Powerful Balboa, carrying the heaviest loads, was happier than he had been for two years.

On the south side of the mountains, they camped by a river that led into the South Sea. There Balboa began building two ships. The ships were almost finished, when a sudden storm made the river overflow its banks. The ships sank. The Spaniards had to climb trees to escape drowning. All their food was washed away.

Balboa did not give up. He had more men, food, and materials brought from Acla. He helped dig the sunken ships from the mud. By May, 1517, they were rebuilt.

Now it was the dry season and the river was too low for the ships to be launched. Channels were scooped out, and the ships were finally set afloat. Men on the river bank cheered. Suddenly the cheers became groans. The ships were sinking. Shipworms had eaten Careta's special wood, just as they ate any wood.

Balboa ordered his men to repair the ships as quickly as possible. The two little ships finally glided down the river and into the sea that Balboa himself had discovered.